The Practicing Witch

witchcraftspellsmagick.com

The Practicing Witch Dream Journal

Witchcraft Spells Magick

Step into a new chapter of self-discovery
and spiritual growth with *The Practicing Witch Dream Journal.*

This journal provides a sacred space to document
your dreams, reflect on recurring symbols, track lucid dreams,
and deepen your understanding of your subconscious.
Use it to explore and record your dream thoughts,
feelings, and experiences, preserving the wisdom
and guidance your dreams offer.

Witchcraft Spells Magick
witchcraftspellsmagick.com
WITCHCRAFT ACADEMY COVEN
Teaching Witches their Craft on Patreon

"Your dreams are your
inner world's secret language,
a spell that unlocks
the wisdom within you."
– *Positive Dreaming Affirmation*

Welcome!

The Practicing Witch Dream Journal is a space to record your thoughts and feelings about your dreams and how you experienced them — a place to preserve your psychic reality.

This journal is not just a place to record nightly visions; it's a sanctuary for your psychic reality, offering a profound connection to your subconscious. Dreams are more than fleeting images —they are potent messengers from deep within, offering insights that can illuminate your path and deepen your self-understanding.

Day Journaling: Begin each day by documenting your dreams, reflecting on their significance to your waking life, and setting intentions influenced by the insights gained, thereby fostering a clearer and more intentional mindset.

Night Journaling: Each evening, set precise intentions for your dreams, review important symbols or themes, and visualize lucid dreaming to strengthen your connection to the subconscious and enhance your nocturnal explorations.

Maintaining a dream journal is a sacred act that enhances memory, boosts self-awareness, and nurtures spiritual growth. As you write down your dreams, you build a bridge between the dream world and your waking reality, inviting clarity, healing, and guidance. Each entry maps your inner journey, reflecting your thoughts, desires, and the profound mysteries beyond your conscious self. Embrace this sacred practice and let your dreams unfold the wisdom you seek.

Blessed Be, Bec Black

The Practicing Witch

© 2025 Copyright Witchcraft Spells Magick

The Practicing Witch Dream Journal
is a Witchcraft Spells Magick publication.
Published by Pagan Publishing
in 2025 for Witchcraft Academy, owned and operated
by Witchcraft Spells Magick.
www.witchcraftspellsmagick.com

Limited Edition DELUXE Hardback ISBN: 978-1-7638843-0-4
Hardback ISBN: 978-1-7638843-1-1
Paperback ISBN: 978-1-7638843-2-8

COVEN: patreon.com/WitchcraftAcademyCoven

YouTube: @WitchMusicPlaylist
Instagram: @witchcraftspellsmagick
Facebook: @witchcraftspellsmagick

Copyright text by Bec Black
Illustrations and original artworks by Bec Black
Additional illustrations sourced through image galleries

All rights reserved.

No part of this publication may be reproduced, stored, or transmitted in any form or by any means, including electronic, mechanical, photocopying, recording, or otherwise, without prior written permission from Witchcraft Spells Magick.

witchcraftspellsmagick.com

Dream Journal

A Coven of Witches
Witchcraft Academy Coven

Become part of an exclusive community of witches in a private space on Patreon.

Whether you're a seasoned practitioner or new to the magickal path, this coven supports and enriches your practice in a welcoming environment.

Membership to the Witchcraft Academy Coven Includes:

A **Welcome Pack with digital resources**
Patreon & Etsy store discount
Monthly Witch Kits filled with new digital resources
Engage in discussions and share insights with like-minded souls
Access to a wealth of **exclusive Practicing Witchcraft digital resources**
Lunar Cycle Reminders with Moon Magick guidance for each phase
Participate in **Coven Tarot Readings** for valuable insights
Post questions and **receive personalized feedback**
Simplify your witchcraft, connect with others, and practice more often

Embrace Your Inner Witch

Join this vibrant community and let your magick flow, welcoming more success and fulfillment into your life. With comprehensive guidance, support, and exclusive content, you'll have everything you need to practice witchcraft and thrive.

Your Invitation Awaits

witchcraftspellsmagick.com/pages/coven

The Practicing Witch

witchcraftspellsmagick.com

Contents
The Practicing Witch Dream Journal

Front Section:

Dream Journaling 0

Five Reasons to Love *The Practicing Witch Dream Journal* 1

How Journaling Works 2-3

Sleep Rituals 5

Introduction 6-7

Daily Rituals 8-9

Dream Recall 10-11

PART 1:

Dreaming Record 12-55

PART 2:

Dream Symbols 56-101

PART 3:

Dream Interpretation 102-153

PART 4:

Dreaming Intentions 154-217

PART 5:

Lucid Dreaming Log 218-251

PART 6:

Creative Dream Flow Journaling 252-299

References 300-301

Dream Journaling

The Practicing Witch Dream Journal is a complete guide to accessing profound insights, offering you wisdom directly from your subconscious.

Are you eager for deeper insight into your dreams and your soul's journey?
Yes/No

Do you feel called to explore the hidden meanings within your subconscious?
Yes/No

Are you ready to dedicate a little time to enhancing your spiritual connection?
Yes/No

If you answered 'yes' to any of these, this journal will guide you through dreamwork, enhancing self-awareness and magick.

Plus there is definitely magick in the process.
You will need to do the work in both your dreams and your waking life.

Step out of your comfort zone.
Embrace your dreams and let them guide you.

This journal is your companion on that journey.
Your guide, your how-to — your passage to spiritual growth.
You are ready.

Five Reasons to Love
The Practicing Witch Dream Journal

1. Unlock the Mysteries of your Dreams
The Practicing Witch Dream Journal invites you
to explore the hidden messages within your dreams.
Each night holds valuable insight, and this journal
offers the space to document and interpret the symbols,
emotions, and messages your subconscious is sending you.

2. Set Intentions for Magickal Clarity
Writing in this journal each morning and evening helps you connect
with your intuition and establish a ritual of intention-setting.
Whether you're seeking guidance, clarity, or manifesting your desires,
it aligns your waking life with the magick of your dreams.

3. A Tool for Personal Growth and Manifestation
By reflecting on your dreams, you invite spiritual growth and transformation.
This journal turns everyday thoughts into magickal experiences,
supporting your journey toward prosperity, peace, and wisdom.

4. Cultivate a Consistent Dream Practice
With dedicated space for both morning reflection and evening
intention-setting, this journal encourages consistency.
It helps you integrate your dreams into your daily spiritual practice,
turning dreamwork into a regular, powerful tool.

5. Empower Your Subconscious Mind
Journaling is a powerful way to tap into your subconscious.
The Practicing Witch Dream Journal helps you unlock your inner wisdom,
explore intuitive insights, and use your dreams as a guide for conscious living.
The more you write, the deeper your connection to your magickal self.

How Journaling Works
Consistency is Key

This journal helps you unlock profound insights by documenting and interpreting the symbols, emotions, and messages from your subconscious. The more you engage, the deeper your connection to your inner wisdom will become. This practice is designed to fit seamlessly into your daily routine, making dream exploration a regular habit.

MORNING ROUTINE
Start your Day with Clarity
Recall your Dream/s

When you wake, take a moment to recall as many dreams as you can from the night before. Don't rush—observe the fragments or full themes that stand out.

Document Emotions, Symbols, and Themes

Write down any emotions you felt, any symbols that were present, or any recurring themes from the dreams. This is a key part of connecting the dream world to your waking life.

Reflect on Connections

Consider how the dream relates to your current situation. Is there something in your waking life that mirrors the dream? Reflect on any personal connections.

Extract Insight

What messages or guidance might the dream be offering you? Take a moment to interpret the dream's meaning and how it can influence your day.

Set your Intention for the Day

Based on the dream's message, set an intention for the day ahead. What action or mindset aligns with the insight you've received? Write it down to keep you grounded throughout the day.

witchcraftspellsmagick.com

By following this simple yet powerful schedule each day, you will turn your dream exploration into a regular, intentional practice. This routine nurtures a deeper connection to your inner wisdom, enhances personal growth, and empowers you to manifest your will with clarity and purpose.

EVENING ROUTINE
Prepare for your Night's Dreamwork
Set your Dream Intention

Before sleep, take a few moments to set an intention for your dreams. Are you seeking clarity on an issue, answers to a question, or a deeper connection to your intuition? State your desire clearly.

Review Dream Symbols or Themes

Take note of any symbols, emotions, or themes from the previous morning's dreams that you want to explore further. This helps maintain your connection to the subconscious.

Journal Thoughts and Feelings

Write down any feelings or thoughts you want to explore in your dreams. This could be a specific question or an unresolved feeling you want to dive into during the night.

Relax and Prepare for Rest

Ease into a restful state and release any tension from the day. Focus on peace and calm, allowing your mind to prepare for the dream journey ahead.

Visualize Lucid Dreaming

Before closing your eyes, visualize yourself becoming aware within a dream. Imagine recognizing the dream state and taking control within it. This prepares your mind for lucid dreaming, enhancing your ability to navigate the dream world consciously.

"I have the ability
to explore my dreams
and learn from them."
– *Positive Dreaming Affirmation*

Sleep Rituals
Your Dream Key

Creating a sleep ritual is key for restful nights and balanced dreams.
This practice sets the stage for peaceful sleep while nurturing your subconscious.
A consistent ritual invites tranquility and clarity into your sleep cycle,
fostering a deeper connection to your inner self.

Night Routine
Prepare Your Body for Rest
Before you sleep, take time to prepare your body and mind.
Create a calming environment—dim the lights,
settle into a comfortable position, and focus on deep, even breaths.

Release Tension
Gently release physical tension with deep breathing,
relaxing muscles from your toes to your head.

Set Your Intention for Rest
Set a clear intention for your night of sleep. What do you want
to experience in your dreams? Whether you seek clarity, peace, or guidance,
verbalize or mentally affirm your desire for restful sleep and insightful dreams.

Reflect and Let Go
Acknowledge the day's events without judgment, then let them go,
trusting your subconscious to process them.

Embrace Calm and Comfort
Close your eyes, visualizing a peaceful scene—a place where you feel completely
relaxed and at ease. Allow your mind to settle into stillness, and trust
that your body is now ready to rest. By establishing this sleep ritual,
you create the foundation for better sleep and deeper dream experiences,
enhancing your well-being and connection to your subconscious.

Introduction
Welcome to your Dream Journal,

Dreams are not merely passing thoughts or fleeting images that cross your mind as you sleep. They are profound messages from the depths of your subconscious, offering a window into greater understanding and self-awareness.

Keeping a dream journal is a sacred practice that enhances memory, deepens self-reflection, and nurtures spiritual growth. By dream journaling each morning, you preserve the fragments that often fade in the rush of daily life. This practice strengthens your connection to your inner self, helping you identify recurring themes, symbols, and emotions—insights that guide you in both everyday and magickal matters.

Through the process of dream journaling, you forge a link between the dream world and your conscious reality, inviting clarity, healing, and direction. Each entry serves as a map of your inner journey, reflecting your thoughts, desires, and the mysteries that lie just beyond your consciousness. Embrace this sacred practice and allow your dreams to offer you the wisdom you seek.

Tips for Effectively Journaling Your Dreams:

1. Write First, Reflect Later

The moment you wake, your dreams are still close,
like the soft fog that lingers at dawn.
Grab your journal and write down everything you can remember, even if it's just a fragment. Don't wait—those details can slip away faster than you think. The key here is speed.
Capture it all before the day rushes in to cloud your mind.

2. Let the Words Flow Freely

Don't censor yourself, and don't worry about perfect writing.
Dreams aren't about neatness—they're about raw, unfiltered truth.
Even if the dream feels odd or uncomfortable, let it flow onto the page.
Every detail, no matter how strange, has a purpose.
Trust the process and let your intuition guide you.

3. Keep It Close, Keep It Sacred

Your dream journal should be as close to you as your altar.
Keep it by your bedside, ready for you as soon as you open your eyes.
In the stillness of the morning, you're connected to the dream realm in ways you can't be during the hustle of the day.
Make it a ritual—gather your thoughts before you gather your to-do list.

4. Write Without Judgment

Dreams are often puzzling, and that's perfectly okay. Don't second-guess them. Don't worry about making sense of everything right away. Sometimes it takes days, weeks, or even months for the meanings to reveal themselves.
Write as if you were an observer, a quiet witness to your own unfolding story.

5. Embrace the Symbols

Not every detail in a dream is literal, and that's where the magic lies. Write down symbols, colors, animals, or emotions that stand out. These are the clues your subconscious is sending. Keep track of what you see, hear, or feel, and allow these symbols to unfold their deeper meanings over time.

6. Make It a Sacred Ritual

The act of dream journaling itself is a sacred ritual. Make it something that feels special, a quiet moment of connection with yourself. Light a candle, sip your morning tea, or simply sit in stillness as you write. Allow the practice to deepen your connection to your own intuition, and open the gateway for even more profound insights.

7. Don't Worry About Perfection

Your dreams are unique to you. They don't need to be polished or neatly organized. This isn't about crafting a perfect narrative —this is about capturing the essence of what your spirit is trying to communicate. Let it be messy, let it be raw, and let it be yours.

Your Sacred Daily Rituals
Ancient & Modern Wisdom tells you...

The beginning and end of your day offer you essential moments for reflection and intention-setting. Why is this important?

Wisdom from both ancient traditions and contemporary practices teaches you that these moments are key to grounding yourself, aligning with your true purpose, and preparing for what lies ahead.

These moments allow you to evaluate, correct course, and prepare for the next step in our journey. Yet, few people have rituals in place that enable them to thrive consistently. These positive habits aren't just for successful entrepreneurs or YouTubers. They are for anyone willing to cultivate them.

Considering logic, it is recommend you keep this journal by your bedside, where it can be easily accessed when you wake up and before you sleep. Let this journal become your first thought when you wake and your final ritual before you fall asleep. You will find that in just a few minutes a day, you'll build powerful habits of mindfulness and reflection. enriching your connection with your dreams and yourself. This ritual requires only a few minutes of your day but is invaluable in establishing a mindset and actions that support your well-being. It's a small effort for a great reward—a reminder to think clearly and act intentionally. Your dreams and subconscious mind are waiting to be explored.

Why you should journal your dreams the moment you wake?

Journaling your dreams immediately upon waking helps capture the details before they fade from memory. It also strengthens your connection to your subconscious, providing valuable insights for personal growth and clarity. By documenting your dreams, you create a lasting record that can reveal recurring patterns and symbols.

What if you could set this tone every day?

The Practicing Witch Dream Journal is designed to help you do just that. Writing in the journal immediately establishes positive habits that impact both your waking life and your dream world.

witchcraftspellsmagick.com

Writing in your journal first thing in the morning, affirmations:
"I trust the wisdom that my dreams offer."
"My dreams guide me toward personal growth and clarity."
"My dreams help me create a positive reality."

Personal growth isn't always comfortable, but it is always rewarding. By writing in your journal, you push past resistance, giving yourself the opportunity to grow spiritually, mentally, and emotionally. You create the foundation for deeper connections, better health, and peaceful sleep.

Why should I dream journal before going to sleep?
What's your usual routine before sleep? Do you find yourself scrolling on your phone or watching TV as the day winds down?

Writing in *The Practicing Witch Dream Journal* before bed is a step towards a more fulfilling, intentional night. Just as brushing your teeth has become a daily habit, so too can writing in your journal be a ritual that nurtures your subconscious and helps you sleep soundly.

Write in your journal last thing in the evening, affirmations:
"I use my dreams to heal and empower myself."
"I remember my dreams every morning with ease."
"My dreams help me create a positive reality."

By writing in your journal before bed, you create a ritual that helps you shift your focus to positivity and gratitude, even when the day hasn't gone as planned. You'll find that this simple habit allows you to sleep a little better and awaken refreshed. In the same way that healthy relationships require consistent effort, your personal growth and spiritual practice benefit from the discipline of writing down your thoughts, dreams, and reflections. This journal invites you to create a consistent habit that enhances your connection to your dreams and subconscious mind.

Dream Recall
Methods and Techniques

Explore these methods to enhance dream recall and strengthen your connection to the messages from your subconscious, opening the door to a world of insight, magick, and self-discovery.

Knowing your own rhythm allows you to plan your dream recall practice around these natural cycles, optimizing your ability to remember your dreams.

Place your Dream Journal Beside your Bed

The most effective method to improve dream recall is to write down your dreams as soon as you wake up. Keep your dream journal within reach, so you can immediately write down details before they slip away. Dream journaling engages your conscious mind and strengthens your connection to the dream world.

Set an Intention Before Sleep

Before going to bed, affirm to yourself that you will remember your dreams. Visualize yourself waking up and recalling your dreams in vivid detail. Setting a clear intention reinforces your subconscious mind's focus on dream recall. A positive affirmation such as, *'I will remember my dreams tonight,'* can help create a powerful connection to your dream memory.

Avoid Moving Immediately Upon Waking

When you wake up, try to stay still for a few moments before opening your eyes or moving your body. Linger in the stillness and let the dream images flow back to your mind. This pause allows your mind to reconnect with the dream world before the distractions of the day take over.

Focus on Feeling Over Detail

If you can't remember all the details of a dream, focus on the feelings you experienced. Was it fear, joy, excitement, or peace? Even if the specific images are lost, capturing the emotions tied to the dream can help you recall more vivid details as you write them down.

Use Dream Triggers

Focus on one element of your dream—a thought, symbol, or feeling—and hold it for a moment. This often triggers more vivid details and, hopefully, the full narrative to surface and unfold in your mind.

Perform Reality Checks Throughout the Day

Reality checks, like looking at your hands or reading text, help train your mind to be more aware of your surroundings. This makes it easier to recognize when you're dreaming and improves dream recall.

Sleep in Complete Darkness

Sleeping in complete darkness helps your body enter deeper sleep cycles, which are often linked to more vivid dreams. It also removes distractions that could interfere with your ability to fully immerse in your dreams, making it easier to recall them upon waking.

Practice Mindfulness and Meditation

Mindfulness throughout the day helps you become more aware of the present moment, enhancing your ability to remember details. Meditation before bed calms your mind and creates space for dream recall. Consider using a relaxation technique, like focusing on your breath, to quiet your thoughts before sleep.

Wake Up During REM Sleep

REM sleep is when the most vivid dreams occur. Ideal for an afternoon nap, set a quiet alarm that gradually gets louder to wake you slower during or just after a REM cycle. Typically, these cycles last about 90 minutes, but shorter naps can still help you catch lighter sleep stages, this practice will lead to clearer and more vivid recollections of your dreams.

Track Your Sleep Patterns

Tracking your sleep patterns can help you understand when you're most likely to dream and how you experience your sleep cycles.

PART 1 | MORNING

Dreaming Record

Dream Visions: Insights and Interpretations

Dreams offer profound insight into your subconscious mind and serve as a valuable tool for personal reflection and magickal practice. Recording your dreams can help you connect with hidden emotions, symbols, and themes that influence your waking life.

How to use your Dreaming Record

Date: Record the date the dream occurred.

Dream Name: A brief name to trigger your memory.

Description/Summary: Use this space to capture the narrative of your dream. Record as many details of your dream as possible, no matter how small. Let the narrative flow and be as descriptive as possible.

Emotional Reaction: Reflect on how you felt during or after the dream. Were you fearful, joyful, confused, or enlightened? How is the dream connected with your current waking emotions?

Themes/Characteristics: Identify any themes, or significant events from the dream (e.g., flying, water, animals), keep track of reoccuring themes and characteristics.

Symbols: What specific symbols stood out in your dream?

Warnings/Toxicity: Were there any warnings or negative feelings related to the dream that might indicate toxicity or danger in your waking life?

Medicinal Use: How the dream can serve as a tool for healing.

Magickal Use: How can the dream themes or symbols be utilized in your magickal practice?

Observations: Additional insights that could aid in understanding your dream?

Dreaming Record *Example*

Date: _3rd March_   Dream Name: _The Blue Butterfly_

Description/Summary: _I was walking through a dense forest when a blue butterfly flew in front of me. It landed on my hand, and as I reached out, the butterfly transformed into a glowing orb. I felt a deep sense of calm and connection to nature as I stepped toward a curved staircase that seemed to beckon me to climb it. I felt that this was a message from the universe._

Emotional Reaction: _I felt peaceful and amazed. There was a sense of wonder and awe, mixed with a deep inner peace._

Themes/Characteristics: _Transformation, Nature, Calm, Change, Healing_

Symbols: _Blue butterfly, Glowing orb, Forest, Light, Stairs_

Warnings/Toxicity: _None identified_

Medicinal Use: _This dream may indicate the need for healing from within, encouraging me to embrace change and new beginnings in my life._

Magickal Use: _The butterfly symbolizes transformation, guiding my personal and magickal growth focusing on renewal and rebirth. I will use butterfly imagery in my rituals to invoke metamorphosis and embrace growth in all areas of my life._

Observations: _I should be open to change and trust the process._

Dream Journal 15

16 The Practicing Witch

witchcraftspellsmagick.com

Dreaming Record

Date: _____ Dream Name: _____

Description/Summary: _____

_____

_____

_____

_____

Emotional Reaction: _____

_____

Themes/Characteristics: _____

_____

Symbols: _____

_____

Warnings/Toxicity: _____

_____

Medicinal Use: _____

_____

Magickal Use: _____

_____

_____

Observations: _____

_____

"The dream
is the small hidden door
in the deepest
and most intimate
sanctum of the soul."
– *C.G. Jung psychiatrist, psychotherapist, and psychologist*

witchcraftspellsmagick.com

Dream Journal

Dreaming Record

Date: _____ Dream Name: _____

Description/Summary: _____

_____

_____

_____

_____

Emotional Reaction: _____

_____

Themes/Characteristics: _____

_____

Symbols: _____

_____

Warnings/Toxicity: _____

_____

Medicinal Use: _____

_____

Magickal Use: _____

_____

Observations: _____

Dreaming Record

Date: _____ Dream Name: _____

Description/Summary: _____

_____

_____

_____

_____

Emotional Reaction: _____

_____

Themes/Characteristics: _____

_____

Symbols: _____

_____

Warnings/Toxicity: _____

_____

Medicinal Use: _____

_____

Magickal Use: _____

_____

_____

Observations: _____

_____

witchcraftspellsmagick.com

Dream Journal

Dreaming Record

Date: _____ Dream Name: _____

Description/Summary: _____

_____

_____

_____

_____

Emotional Reaction: _____

_____

Themes/Characteristics: _____

_____

Symbols: _____

_____

Warnings/Toxicity: _____

_____

Medicinal Use: _____

_____

Magickal Use: _____

_____

_____

Observations: _____

_____

"But it was all a dream;
no Eve soothed my sorrows
nor shared my thoughts;
I was alone.
I remembered Adam's
supplication to his Creator.
But where was mine?
He had abandoned me,
and in the bitterness
of my heart I cursed him."

– *Mary Wollstonecraft Shelley author Frankenstein*

witchcraftspellsmagick.com

Dreaming Record

Date: _____ Dream Name: _____

Description/Summary: _____

_____

_____

_____

_____

Emotional Reaction: _____

_____

Themes/Characteristics: _____

_____

Symbols: _____

_____

Warnings/Toxicity: _____

_____

Medicinal Use: _____

_____

Magickal Use: _____

_____

Observations: _____

Dreaming Record

Date: _____ Dream Name: _____

Description/Summary: _____

_____

_____

_____

_____

Emotional Reaction: _____

_____

Themes/Characteristics: _____

_____

Symbols: _____

_____

Warnings/Toxicity: _____

_____

Medicinal Use: _____

_____

Magickal Use: _____

_____

_____

Observations: _____

_____

witchcraftspellsmagick.com

Dreaming Record

Date: _____ Dream Name: _____

Description/Summary: _____

_____

_____

_____

_____

Emotional Reaction: _____

_____

Themes/Characteristics: _____

_____

Symbols: _____

_____

Warnings/Toxicity: _____

_____

Medicinal Use: _____

_____

Magickal Use: _____

_____

Observations: _____

_____

"Dreams are the whispers of your soul, revealing the hidden truths that the waking mind may not see."
– *Positive Dreaming Affirmation*

Dream Journal 35

Dreaming Record

Date: _____ Dream Name: _____

Description/Summary: _____

_____

_____

_____

_____

Emotional Reaction: _____

_____

Themes/Characteristics: _____

_____

Symbols: _____

_____

Warnings/Toxicity: _____

_____

Medicinal Use: _____

_____

Magickal Use: _____

_____

Observations: _____

_____

Dreaming Record

Date: _____ Dream Name: _____

Description/Summary: _____

_____

_____

_____

Emotional Reaction: _____

_____

Themes/Characteristics: _____

_____

Symbols: _____

_____

Warnings/Toxicity: _____

_____

Medicinal Use: _____

_____

Magickal Use: _____

_____

Observations: _____

_____

Dream Journal 39

witchcraftspellsmagick.com

Dreaming Record

Date: _____ Dream Name: _____

Description/Summary: _____

_____

_____

_____

_____

Emotional Reaction: _____

_____

Themes/Characteristics: _____

_____

Symbols: _____

_____

Warnings/Toxicity: _____

_____

Medicinal Use: _____

_____

Magickal Use: _____

_____

_____

Observations: _____

_____

"A dreamer,
I walked enchanted,
and nothing held me back."
– Daphne du Maurier *author Rebecca*

witchcraftspellsmagick.com

witchcraftspellsmagick.com

Dreaming Record

Date: _____ Dream Name: _____

Description/Summary: _____

_____

_____

_____

_____

Emotional Reaction: _____

_____

Themes/Characteristics: _____

_____

Symbols: _____

_____

Warnings/Toxicity: _____

_____

Medicinal Use: _____

_____

Magickal Use: _____

_____

Observations: _____

_____

Dreaming Record

Date: _____ Dream Name: _____

Description/Summary: _____

_____

_____

_____

Emotional Reaction: _____

_____

Themes/Characteristics: _____

_____

Symbols: _____

_____

Warnings/Toxicity: _____

_____

Medicinal Use: _____

_____

Magickal Use: _____

_____

Observations: _____

_____

Dreaming Record

Date: _____ Dream Name: _____

Description/Summary: _____

Emotional Reaction: _____

Themes/Characteristics: _____

Symbols: _____

Warnings/Toxicity: _____

Medicinal Use: _____

Magickal Use: _____

Observations: _____

"And when he awoke
in the morning and looked upon
the wretchedness about him,
his dream had had its usual effect:
it had intensified the sordidness
of his surroundings a thousandfold."
– Mark Twain *author Prince and the Pauper*

Dreaming Record

Date: _____ Dream Name: _____

Description/Summary: _____

_____

_____

_____

_____

Emotional Reaction: _____

_____

Themes/Characteristics: _____

_____

Symbols: _____

_____

Warnings/Toxicity: _____

_____

Medicinal Use: _____

_____

Magickal Use: _____

_____

_____

Observations: _____

_____

witchcraftspellsmagick.com

Dream Journal 53

Dreaming Record

Date: _____ Dream Name: _____

Description/Summary: _____

_____

_____

_____

_____

Emotional Reaction: _____

_____

Themes/Characteristics: _____

_____

Symbols: _____

_____

Warnings/Toxicity: _____

_____

Medicinal Use: _____

_____

Magickal Use: _____

_____

_____

Observations: _____

_____

PART 2 | MORNING

Dream Symbols
Deciphering Dream Symbolism

"Symbols are the language of the soul."
This section is designed for recording and interpreting the recurring symbols that appear in your dreams. Symbols are powerful tools in dreamwork, often carrying deep meanings that can provide insight into your emotional, spiritual, and personal life. They offer a direct connection to the subconscious mind and can serve as guides in your waking world.

By reflecting on the symbols you encounter, you can begin to understand their personal significance and the messages they convey. Each symbol may carry a universal meaning, but it is also important to consider how it resonates with your unique experiences and circumstances.

The more you engage with your dreams and the symbols within them, the more you will uncover layers of hidden wisdom that can help you navigate life's challenges. Keep an open mind, and allow your intuition to guide you as you work with these symbols.

Recommended Reading:
'The Dreamer's Dictionary' by Stearn Robinson & Tom Corbett
'Man and His Symbols' by Carl G. Jung
'Dreams: A Portal to the Source' by Edward C. Whitmont
'Women's Symbols' by Barbara Walker

Dream Symbols *Example*

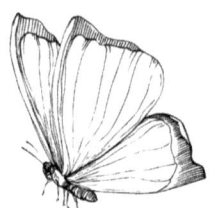

Symbol: *Butterfly*

Meaning/Interpretation: *Transformation and personal growth. A symbol of change, evolution, and rebirth. Freedom and lightness of being. Spiritual awakening or a deeper connection to the soul. A reminder to embrace change with grace.*

Mystical Meaning: *Represents the soul's journey and cycles of life, death, and rebirth. Often associated with the element of air, symbolizing intellectual transformation. A sign to embrace the new phase of life.*

Personal Insight: *The butterfly represents the changes I'm currently going through, particularly in my career and personal life. It reminds me that growth takes time and that I must trust the process.*

Symbol: *Stairs*

Meaning/Interpretation: *A journey or a transition. Ascending stairs might suggest progress or advancement, symbolizing achievements or a movement toward higher awareness or understanding.*

Meaning/Interpretation: *Stairs symbolize ascension to higher knowledge and realms, representing a journey that requires effort and gradual steps toward wisdom.*

Personal Insight: *Stairs often appear in my dreams when I'm faced with a decision or challenge that requires effort to overcome. It reminds me that each step forward, no matter how small, is progress.*

Dream Symbols

Symbol: _____

Meaning/Interpretation: _____

Mystical Meaning: _____

Personal Insight: _____

Symbol: _____

Meaning/Interpretation: _____

Meaning/Interpretation: _____

Personal Insight: _____

Dream Journal

Symbol: _____

Meaning/Interpretation: _____
_____
_____
_____
_____

Mystical Meaning: _____
_____
_____
_____
_____

Personal Insight: _____
_____
_____
_____
_____

Symbol: _____

Meaning/Interpretation: _____
_____
_____
_____
_____

Meaning/Interpretation: _____
_____
_____
_____
_____

Personal Insight: _____
_____
_____
_____
_____

Dream Symbols

Symbol: _____

Meaning/Interpretation: _____

Mystical Meaning: _____

Personal Insight: _____

Symbol: _____

Meaning/Interpretation: _____

Meaning/Interpretation: _____

Personal Insight: _____

Dream Journal 63

Dream Symbols

	Meaning/Interpretation: _____
	_____
	_____
	_____
	_____
Symbol: _____	_____
Mystical Meaning: _____	Personal Insight: _____
_____	_____
_____	_____
_____	_____
_____	_____

	Meaning/Interpretation: _____
	_____
	_____
	_____
	_____
Symbol: _____	_____
Meaning/Interpretation: _____	Personal Insight: _____
_____	_____
_____	_____
_____	_____
_____	_____

Dream Symbols

Symbol: _____

Meaning/Interpretation: _____

Mystical Meaning: _____

Personal Insight: _____

Symbol: _____

Meaning/Interpretation: _____

Meaning/Interpretation: _____

Personal Insight: _____

Dream Journal

	Meaning/Interpretation:
Symbol:	
Mystical Meaning:	Personal Insight:

	Meaning/Interpretation:
Symbol:	
Meaning/Interpretation:	Personal Insight:

Dream Symbols

Symbol: _____

Meaning/Interpretation: _____

Mystical Meaning: _____

Personal Insight: _____

Symbol: _____

Meaning/Interpretation: _____

Meaning/Interpretation: _____

Personal Insight: _____

Dream Journal

Dream Symbols

Symbol:	Meaning/Interpretation:
Mystical Meaning:	Personal Insight:

Symbol:	Meaning/Interpretation:
Meaning/Interpretation:	Personal Insight:

Dream Symbols

Symbol:

Meaning/Interpretation:

Mystical Meaning:

Personal Insight:

Symbol:

Meaning/Interpretation:

Meaning/Interpretation:

Personal Insight:

Dream Journal

Symbol:	Meaning/Interpretation:
Mystical Meaning:	Personal Insight:

Symbol:	Meaning/Interpretation:
Meaning/Interpretation:	Personal Insight:

Dream Symbols

Symbol: _____

Meaning/Interpretation: _____

Mystical Meaning: _____

Personal Insight: _____

Symbol: _____

Meaning/Interpretation: _____

Meaning/Interpretation: _____

Personal Insight: _____

Dream Symbols

Symbol: _____

Meaning/Interpretation: _____

Mystical Meaning: _____

Personal Insight: _____

Symbol: _____

Meaning/Interpretation: _____

Meaning/Interpretation: _____

Personal Insight: _____

Dream Symbols

Symbol: _____

Meaning/Interpretation: _____

Mystical Meaning: _____

Personal Insight: _____

Symbol: _____

Meaning/Interpretation: _____

Meaning/Interpretation: _____

Personal Insight: _____

Symbol:	Meaning/Interpretation:
Mystical Meaning:	Personal Insight:

Symbol:	Meaning/Interpretation:
Meaning/Interpretation:	Personal Insight:

Dream Symbols

Symbol: _____

Meaning/Interpretation: _____

Mystical Meaning: _____

Personal Insight: _____

Symbol: _____

Meaning/Interpretation: _____

Meaning/Interpretation: _____

Personal Insight: _____

Dream Symbols

Symbol:	Meaning/Interpretation:
Mystical Meaning:	Personal Insight:

Symbol:	Meaning/Interpretation:
Meaning/Interpretation:	Personal Insight:

Dream Symbols

Symbol: _____

Meaning/Interpretation: _____

Mystical Meaning: _____

Personal Insight: _____

Symbol: _____

Meaning/Interpretation: _____

Meaning/Interpretation: _____

Personal Insight: _____

Symbol: _____

Meaning/Interpretation: _____
_____
_____
_____
_____

Mystical Meaning: _____
_____
_____
_____
_____

Personal Insight: _____
_____
_____
_____
_____

Symbol: _____

Meaning/Interpretation: _____
_____
_____
_____
_____

Meaning/Interpretation: _____
_____
_____
_____
_____

Personal Insight: _____
_____
_____
_____
_____

Dream Symbols

Symbol: _____

Meaning/Interpretation: _____
_____
_____
_____
_____

Mystical Meaning: _____
_____
_____
_____
_____

Personal Insight: _____
_____
_____
_____
_____

Symbol: _____

Meaning/Interpretation: _____
_____
_____
_____
_____

Meaning/Interpretation: _____
_____
_____
_____
_____

Personal Insight: _____
_____
_____
_____
_____

Dream Journal

Dream Symbols

	Meaning/Interpretation:
Symbol:	
Mystical Meaning:	Personal Insight:

	Meaning/Interpretation:
Symbol:	
Meaning/Interpretation:	Personal Insight:

Dream Symbols

Symbol: _____

Meaning/Interpretation: _____

Mystical Meaning: _____

Personal Insight: _____

Symbol: _____

Meaning/Interpretation: _____

Meaning/Interpretation: _____

Personal Insight: _____

Dream Journal

Symbol: _____

Meaning/Interpretation: _____
_____
_____
_____

Mystical Meaning: _____
_____
_____
_____
_____

Personal Insight: _____
_____
_____
_____
_____

Symbol: _____

Meaning/Interpretation: _____
_____
_____
_____

Meaning/Interpretation: _____
_____
_____
_____
_____

Personal Insight: _____
_____
_____
_____
_____

Dream Symbols

Symbol: _____

Meaning/Interpretation: _____

Mystical Meaning: _____

Personal Insight: _____

Symbol: _____

Meaning/Interpretation: _____

Meaning/Interpretation: _____

Personal Insight: _____

Dream Journal

Dream Symbols

	Meaning/Interpretation: _____
Symbol: _____	
Mystical Meaning: _____	Personal Insight: _____

	Meaning/Interpretation: _____
Symbol: _____	
Meaning/Interpretation: _____	Personal Insight: _____

Dream Symbols

Symbol: _____

Meaning/Interpretation: _____
_____
_____
_____
_____

Mystical Meaning: _____
_____
_____
_____
_____

Personal Insight: _____
_____
_____
_____
_____

Symbol: _____

Meaning/Interpretation: _____
_____
_____
_____
_____

Meaning/Interpretation: _____
_____
_____
_____
_____

Personal Insight: _____
_____
_____
_____
_____

Dream Journal

Symbol: _____

Mystical Meaning: _____

Meaning/Interpretation: _____

Personal Insight: _____

Symbol: _____

Meaning/Interpretation: _____

Meaning/Interpretation: _____

Personal Insight: _____

Dream Symbols

Symbol: _____

Meaning/Interpretation: _____

Mystical Meaning: _____

Personal Insight: _____

Symbol: _____

Meaning/Interpretation: _____

Meaning/Interpretation: _____

Personal Insight: _____

Dream Journal

Dream Symbols

Symbol: _____

Meaning/Interpretation: _____

Mystical Meaning: _____

Personal Insight: _____

Symbol: _____

Meaning/Interpretation: _____

Meaning/Interpretation: _____

Personal Insight: _____

PART 3 | MORNING

Dream Interpretation
Decoding your Dream Messages

Dream interpretation is a powerful tool for self-discovery and understanding. Whether you're reflecting on how your dreams connect to your waking life or exploring symbolic meanings through dream dictionaries or spiritual resources, this is where you can uncover the deeper layers of your subconscious. The following space is for deep reflection and interpretation of dreams, whether through personal insights or external sources.

How to use your Dreaming Interpretation

Date: Record the date the dream occurred.

Dream Name: A brief name to trigger your memory.

Description/Summary: Use this space to capture the narrative of your dream. Record as many details of your dream as possible, no matter how small. Let the narrative flow and be as descriptive as possible.

Symbols: What specific symbols stood out in your dream?

Resource: Dream dictionaries, spiritual guides, or other resources.

Resource Guidance: This section offers space to record references and meanings from dream dictionaries, spiritual guides, or other resources. Expanding your dream vocabulary can help you interpret the messages your dreams are sending you.

Recommended Reading:

'The Complete Dictionary of Dreams' by Dr. Michael Lennox

'The Dreamer's Dictionary' by Stearn Robinson & Tom Corbett

'Dreams and Spirituality: A Guide to the Soul's Journey' by John A. Sanford

'The Witch's Book of Dreams' by Rose Vanden Eynden

Dreaming Interpretation *Example*

Date: 3rd March   Dream Name: The Blue Butterfly

Description/Summary: I was walking through a dense forest when a blue butterfly flew in front of me. It landed on my hand, and as I reached out, the butterfly transformed into a glowing orb. I felt a deep sense of calm and connection to nature as I stepped toward a curved staircase that seemed to beckon me to climb it. I felt that this was a message from the universe.

Symbols: Blue butterfly, Glowing orb, Forest, Light, Stairs

Resources: The Dreamer's Dictionary by Stearn Robinson & Tom Corbett
Guidance from meditation or dream journaling
Dream insight from tarot reading during nature-based ritual

Guidance from Resources: A glowing orb might symbolize spiritual messages and divine guidance. It can also represent clarity and insight, suggesting a connection to the spiritual realm. The forest may signify grounding, nature's nurturing energy, and personal transformation. Light often symbolizes enlightenment, clarity, and hidden truths, guiding the dreamer toward awakening and self-discovery.

Thoughts and Feelings: As the blue butterfly landed on my hand, a quiet realization settled over me—I felt as though I was being acknowledged by something greater than myself. When it transformed into a glowing orb, a deep sense of wonder and reassurance filled me, as if I was receiving an unspoken message of guidance. The staircase ahead felt like an invitation, stirring both curiosity and anticipation.

witchcraftspellsmagick.com

Dreaming Interpretation

Date: _____ Dream Name: _____

Description/Summary: _____

_____

_____

_____

_____

Symbols: _____

Resources: _____

_____

_____

Guidance from Resources: _____

_____

_____

_____

_____

Thoughts and Feelings: _____

_____

_____

_____

Dreaming Interpretation

Date: _____ Dream Name: _____

Description/Summary: _____

_____

_____

_____

_____

Symbols: _____

Resources: _____

_____

Guidance from Resources: _____

_____

_____

_____

_____

Thoughts and Feelings: _____

_____

_____

_____

witchcraftspellsmagick.com

Dreaming Interpretation

Date: _____ Dream Name: _____

Description/Summary: _____

_____

_____

_____

_____

Symbols: _____

Resources: _____

_____

_____

Guidance from Resources: _____

_____

_____

_____

_____

Thoughts and Feelings: _____

_____

_____

_____

Dreaming Interpretation

Date: _____ Dream Name: _____

Description/Summary: _____

_____
_____
_____
_____

Symbols: _____

Resources: _____

_____
_____

Guidance from Resources: _____

_____
_____
_____
_____

Thoughts and Feelings: _____

_____
_____
_____

"For the soul,
when it is separated
from the body,
is not in the state
of being asleep,
but of being awake."

– *Plato philosopher author Phaedo, 68c*

witchcraftspellsmagick.com

Dreaming Interpretation

Date: _____ Dream Name: _____

Description/Summary: _____

_____

_____

_____

_____

Symbols: _____

Resources: _____

_____

Guidance from Resources: _____

_____

_____

_____

_____

Thoughts and Feelings: _____

_____

_____

_____

Dreaming Interpretation

Date: _____ Dream Name: _____

Description/Summary: _____

_____

_____

_____

_____

Symbols: _____

Resources: _____

_____

Guidance from Resources: _____

_____

_____

_____

_____

Thoughts and Feelings: _____

_____

_____

_____

Dream Journal

Dreaming Interpretation

Date: _____ Dream Name: _____

Description/Summary: _____

_____

_____

_____

_____

Symbols: _____

Resources: _____

_____

Guidance from Resources: _____

_____

_____

_____

_____

Thoughts and Feelings: _____

_____

_____

_____

Dreaming Interpretation

Date: _____ Dream Name: _____

Description/Summary: _____

Symbols: _____

Resources: _____

Guidance from Resources: _____

Thoughts and Feelings: _____

Dream Journal 121

"We are the music makers,
and we are the dreamers
of dreams."

– *Roald Dahl author Charlie and the Chocolate Factory*

witchcraftspellsmagick.com

Dreaming Interpretation

Date: _____ Dream Name: _____

Description/Summary: _____

_____

_____

_____

Symbols: _____

Resources: _____

_____

_____

Guidance from Resources: _____

_____

_____

_____

_____

Thoughts and Feelings: _____

_____

_____

_____

Dreaming Interpretation

Date: _____ Dream Name: _____

Description/Summary: _____

_____

_____

_____

_____

Symbols: _____

Resources: _____

_____

Guidance from Resources: _____

_____

_____

_____

_____

Thoughts and Feelings: _____

_____

_____

Dream Journal 125

Dreaming Interpretation

Date: _____ Dream Name: _____

Description/Summary: _____

_____

_____

_____

_____

Symbols: _____

Resources: _____

_____

_____

Guidance from Resources: _____

_____

_____

_____

_____

_____

Thoughts and Feelings: _____

_____

_____

_____

Dreaming Interpretation

Date: _____ Dream Name: _____

Description/Summary: _____

_____
_____
_____
_____

Symbols: _____

Resources: _____

_____
_____

Guidance from Resources: _____

_____
_____
_____
_____

Thoughts and Feelings: _____

_____
_____
_____

"Deep into that darkness peering,
long I stood there, wondering,
fearing, doubting, dreaming dreams
no mortal ever dared to dream before."

– *Edgar Allan Poe author The Raven*

Dreaming Interpretation

Date: _____ Dream Name: _____

Description/Summary: _____

Symbols: _____

Resources: _____

Guidance from Resources: _____

Thoughts and Feelings: _____

Dreaming Interpretation

Date: _____ Dream Name: _____

Description/Summary: _____

_____
_____
_____
_____

Symbols: _____

Resources: _____

_____
_____

Guidance from Resources: _____

_____
_____
_____
_____
_____

Thoughts and Feelings: _____

_____
_____
_____
_____

Dream Journal

witchcraftspellsmagick.com

Dreaming Interpretation

Date: _____ Dream Name: _____

Description/Summary: _____

_____

_____

_____

_____

Symbols: _____

Resources: _____

_____

_____

Guidance from Resources: _____

_____

_____

_____

_____

_____

Thoughts and Feelings: _____

_____

_____

_____

Dreaming Interpretation

Date: _____ Dream Name: _____

Description/Summary: _____

_____

_____

_____

_____

Symbols: _____

Resources: _____

_____

_____

Guidance from Resources: _____

_____

_____

_____

_____

Thoughts and Feelings: _____

_____

_____

_____

Dreaming Interpretation

Date: _____ Dream Name: _____

Description/Summary: _____

_____
_____
_____
_____

Symbols: _____

Resources: _____

_____
_____

Guidance from Resources: _____

_____
_____
_____
_____
_____

Thoughts and Feelings: _____

_____
_____
_____

Dreaming Intentions

Date: _____ Dream Intention: _____

1. What is your intention for tonight's dream, what insights do you seek? _____

_____
_____
_____
_____
_____

2. What questions do you want your dream to answer? _____

_____
_____
_____
_____

3. What method can you use to increase dream awareness or lucidity? _____

_____
_____
_____
_____

4. How can your dreams guide your personal growth or transformation? _____

_____
_____
_____
_____

5. How will you reflect on your dreams upon waking? _____

_____
_____
_____

witchcraftspellsmagick.com

"If you have built castles in the air,
your work need not be lost;
that is where they should be.
Now put the foundations under them."

– *Henry David Thoreau author Walden*

witchcraftspellsmagick.com

Dreaming Interpretation

Date: _____ Dream Name: _____

Description/Summary: _____

Symbols: _____

Resources: _____

Guidance from Resources: _____

Thoughts and Feelings: _____

Dreaming Interpretation

Date: _____ Dream Name: _____

Description/Summary: _____

_____

_____

_____

_____

Symbols: _____

Resources: _____

_____

Guidance from Resources: _____

_____

_____

_____

_____

Thoughts and Feelings: _____

_____

_____

_____

_____

Dreaming Interpretation

Date: _____ Dream Name: _____

Description/Summary: _____

_____

_____

_____

Symbols: _____

Resources: _____

_____

_____

Guidance from Resources: _____

_____

_____

_____

_____

Thoughts and Feelings: _____

_____

_____

_____

Dream Journal

Dreaming Interpretation

Date: _____ Dream Name: _____

Description/Summary: _____

_____

_____

_____

_____

Symbols: _____

Resources: _____

_____

Guidance from Resources: _____

_____

_____

_____

_____

Thoughts and Feelings: _____

_____

_____

_____

Dreaming Interpretation

Date: _____ Dream Name: _____

Description/Summary: _____

_____

_____

_____

_____

Symbols: _____

Resources: _____

_____

_____

Guidance from Resources: _____

_____

_____

_____

_____

Thoughts and Feelings: _____

_____

_____

_____

Dream Journal   151

Dreaming Interpretation

Date: _____ Dream Name: _____

Description/Summary: _____

_____

_____

_____

_____

Symbols: _____

Resources: _____

_____

Guidance from Resources: _____

_____

_____

_____

_____

Thoughts and Feelings: _____

_____

_____

_____

PART 4 | EVENING
Dreaming Intentions
Dreaming with Purpose

Setting clear intentions for your dreaming state empowers you to guide your dreams toward deeper insights, personal growth, and spiritual exploration. This section offers prompts to help you set purposeful, focused intentions for your dreams. By journaling and visualizing before sleep, you can invite specific themes, emotions, or symbols into your dreams. These practices help you engage and deepen your experience with the dream world, creating meaningful experiences that align with your personal growth.

How to Set Intentions for your Dreams

Date: Record the date the intention was set.

Dream Intention: Write your main intention for tonight's dream —what you wish to experience or learn.

Why is this your main intention for tonight's dream? What insights do you seek? Reflect on why this intention feels important to you at this time.

What questions do you want your dream to answer? Use this space to specify any questions or concerns you wish to explore in your dreams.

What method can you use to increase dream awareness or lucidity? Note techniques you will use to help you stay aware or lucid in your dreams, such as reality checks, affirmations, or breathwork.

What area of personal growth or transformation could your dreams offer wisdom? Focus on a specific area of your life where you seek guidance, healing, or personal development through your dreams.

How will you reflect on your dreams upon waking? Plan how you will document your dreams and any insights gained after waking up.

Dreaming with Intention
Your Pathway for Deeper Connection to Self

Setting clear intentions for your dreaming state will empower you to shape your dreams and gain insights for personal growth. By actively preparing yourself for the dream world, you can create a pathway for deeper connection, guidance, and transformation during your sleep.

Affirmations

Repeating a mantra, such as *"I will have vivid, insightful dreams,"* or *"I will remember my dreams clearly,"* before sleep strengthens your commitment to your dream intentions. Affirmations can help imprint these desires into your subconscious, making them more likely to manifest.

Breath Work

Deep, calming breathwork before sleep helps ground your mind and body's energy. Belly breathing or alternate nostril breathing work to clear both mental clutter and enhance your focus, making it easier to stay connected to your intention.

Dream Incubation

Dream incubation involves focusing on a specific question or intention before you sleep. As you drift off, hold the intention in your mind and ask for guidance or answers through your dreams. This practice will encourage relevant, insightful dreams connected to your waking goals.

Dream Symbols

Focus on a symbol or theme before you sleep that you'd like to appear in your dreams. Whether it's a specific object, animal, or idea, envision this in a symbol form, entering your dream space. By setting this intention, you invite the symbol to guide your dream exploration.

Energy Work

Before you sleep, focus on raising and directing your energy. Use visualization or movement to activate your energy centers, so that you carry this heightened awareness into your dreams. This practice can enhance the intensity and clarity of your dream experiences.

Intuitive Dreaming

Talk to your subconscious before sleep, and ask it to provide insights into a specific area of your life—whether personal growth, relationships, or spiritual questions. Set an intention to receive intuitive guidance with clairty during your dreams.

Journaling

Keeping a dream journal helps strengthen the connection between your waking life and your dream state. Writing your intentions in the journal before sleep reinforces your commitment, and it also offers a way to track recurring symbols, patterns, or insights from your dreams.

Meditation

Meditation before sleep clears your mind, allowing you to set clear, focused intentions for the night ahead. Through mindfulness meditation, you prepare your subconscious to engage with your dreams. Increasing your chances of achieving your intentions within them. Meditation helps create a peaceful mental state that fosters clarity and openness, allowing you to connect more deeply with your inner self during your dreams.

Mnemonic Induction of Lucid Dreams (MILD)

As you fall asleep, repeat the phrase *"I will recognize when I am dreaming"* while visualizing yourself becoming lucid in a dream. This technique helps train your mind to recognize when you're in the dream state, making it easier to take control and follow through with your intended experiences.

Reality Checks

Making a habit of reality checks throughout the day trains your mind to stay alert during your dreams. Look at your hands, read a piece of text, or push a finger through your palm to check if you're dreaming. These small actions help you develop awareness that you can carry into your dreams.

Rituals

Creating a pre-sleep ritual, such as listening to nature sounds, performing a short meditation, or casting a protective circle, sets the stage for your dreaming practice. Rituals signal to your subconscious that you are about to enter a sacred, intentional space for dream exploration. These acts help transition your mind and body into a receptive state, fostering deeper dream experiences.

Self-Hypnosis

Inducing a light trance or using self-hypnosis can prime your mind to enter a more focused, intentional dream state. These techniques enhance awareness and help you stay aligned with your goals, ensuring your dreams support your waking-life intentions.

Sleep Environment

Create an optimal sleep environment that supports your dreaming intentions. When ready for sleep, make sure the room is dark and free from distractions, with no sounds or devices, to help you enter a deeper sleep state.

Visualization

Use visualization to imagine the dream experiences you want to have. Picture your desired dreams in vivid detail before you fall asleep. This process helps direct your mind's focus, encouraging specific themes, symbols, or scenarios to manifest during your sleep. Visualizing your dreams with intention creates a powerful mental pathway that guides your subconscious during the night.

Wake-Back-to-Bed (WBTB)

Wake up after a few hours of sleep, stay awake for 20-30 minutes, and then return to sleep. This technique increases the likelihood of entering REM sleep, which is when vivid, lucid, and intentional dreams are most likely to occur.

Dreaming Intentions
Not sure where to begin? Start here.

Setting intentions for your dreams can be a powerful tool to guide your subconscious mind and deepen your personal growth. Try these steps first to unlock the potential of your dreams and gain meaningful *'intentional'* insights.

Set an Intention: Before bed, decide what you want to explore, understand, or manifest in your dreams.

Focus on the Intention: Visualize your desired outcome or focus on a symbol you'd like to appear.

Affirmation Practice: Repeat your intention aloud or in your mind to solidify it in your subconscious.

Dream Journal: Write down your experience after waking up, reflecting on any messages, symbols, or insights you received.

Dreaming Intentions *Example*

Date: _3rd March_   Dream Intention: _To find clarity on my career direction_

1. What is your intention for tonight's dream, what insights do you seek?
Why is this your main intention for tonight's dream? What insights do you seek? I've been feeling uncertain about my career path lately, and I want to receive guidance on whether I should pursue a new opportunity or continue on my current path. I hope my dream provides insight into what aligns best with my values and passions.

2. What questions do you want your dream to answer? _Should I stay in my current job, or is it time for a change? How can I align my work life with my true purpose?_

3. What method can you use to increase dream awareness or lucidity? _I will repeat the affirmation "I will recognize when I am dreaming" before bed. I'll also practice reality checks during the day, like looking at my hands and asking myself, "Am I dreaming?"_

4. How can your dreams guide your personal growth or transformation?
I am seeking wisdom on trusting my intuition and making bold decisions. I would like my dreams to guide me in embracing change and taking steps toward a more fulfilling and purpose-driven career.

5. How will you reflect on your dreams upon waking? _I will immediately write down the dream details in my journal, paying special attention to any symbols and themes._

Dreaming Intentions

Date: _____ Dream Intention: _____

1. What is your intention for tonight's dream, what insights do you seek? _____

_____

_____

_____

2. What questions do you want your dream to answer? _____

_____

_____

3. What method can you use to increase dream awareness or lucidity? _____

_____

_____

4. How can your dreams guide your personal growth or transformation? _____

_____

_____

5. How will you reflect on your dreams upon waking? _____

_____

_____

Dreaming Intentions

Date: _____ Dream Intention: _____

1. What is your intention for tonight's dream, what insights do you seek? _____

_____

_____

_____

2. What questions do you want your dream to answer? _____

_____

_____

3. What method can you use to increase dream awareness or lucidity? _____

_____

_____

4. How can your dreams guide your personal growth or transformation? _____

_____

_____

5. How will you reflect on your dreams upon waking? _____

_____

_____

Dreaming Intentions

Date: _____ Dream Intention: _____

1. What is your intention for tonight's dream, what insights do you seek? _____

_____

_____

_____

2. What questions do you want your dream to answer? _____

_____

_____

_____

3. What method can you use to increase dream awareness or lucidity? _____

_____

_____

_____

4. How can your dreams guide your personal growth or transformation? _____

_____

_____

_____

5. How will you reflect on your dreams upon waking? _____

_____

_____

Dream Journal

Dreaming Intentions

Date: _____ Dream Intention: _____

1. What is your intention for tonight's dream, what insights do you seek? _____

_____

_____

_____

2. What questions do you want your dream to answer? _____

_____

_____

_____

3. What method can you use to increase dream awareness or lucidity? _____

_____

_____

_____

4. How can your dreams guide your personal growth or transformation? _____

_____

_____

_____

5. How will you reflect on your dreams upon waking? _____

_____

_____

Dreaming Intentions

Date: _____ Dream Intention: _____

1. What is your intention for tonight's dream, what insights do you seek? _____

_____
_____
_____
_____

2. What questions do you want your dream to answer? _____

_____
_____
_____

3. What method can you use to increase dream awareness or lucidity? _____

_____
_____
_____

4. How can your dreams guide your personal growth or transformation? _____

_____
_____
_____

5. How will you reflect on your dreams upon waking? _____

_____
_____

witchcraftspellsmagick.com

Dreaming Intentions

Date: _____ Dream Intention: _____

1. What is your intention for tonight's dream, what insights do you seek? _____

_____

_____

_____

2. What questions do you want your dream to answer? _____

_____

_____

_____

3. What method can you use to increase dream awareness or lucidity? _____

_____

_____

_____

4. How can your dreams guide your personal growth or transformation? _____

_____

_____

_____

5. How will you reflect on your dreams upon waking? _____

_____

_____

Dreaming Intentions

Date: _____ Dream Intention: _____

1. What is your intention for tonight's dream, what insights do you seek? _____

_____

_____

_____

_____

2. What questions do you want your dream to answer? _____

_____

_____

_____

3. What method can you use to increase dream awareness or lucidity? _____

_____

_____

_____

4. How can your dreams guide your personal growth or transformation? _____

_____

_____

_____

5. How will you reflect on your dreams upon waking? _____

_____

_____

Dreaming Intentions

Date: _____ Dream Intention: _____

1. What is your intention for tonight's dream, what insights do you seek? _____

_____

_____

_____

2. What questions do you want your dream to answer? _____

_____

_____

_____

3. What method can you use to increase dream awareness or lucidity? _____

_____

_____

_____

4. How can your dreams guide your personal growth or transformation? _____

_____

_____

_____

5. How will you reflect on your dreams upon waking? _____

_____

Dreaming Intentions

Date: _____ Dream Intention: _____

1. What is your intention for tonight's dream, what insights do you seek? _____

_____

_____

_____

_____

2. What questions do you want your dream to answer? _____

_____

_____

_____

3. What method can you use to increase dream awareness or lucidity? _____

_____

_____

_____

4. How can your dreams guide your personal growth or transformation? _____

_____

_____

_____

5. How will you reflect on your dreams upon waking? _____

_____

_____

Dreaming Intentions

Date: _____ Dream Intention: _____

1. What is your intention for tonight's dream, what insights do you seek? _____

2. What questions do you want your dream to answer? _____

3. What method can you use to increase dream awareness or lucidity? _____

4. How can your dreams guide your personal growth or transformation? _____

5. How will you reflect on your dreams upon waking? _____

Dreaming Intentions

Date: _____ Dream Intention: _____

1. What is your intention for tonight's dream, what insights do you seek? _____

_____

_____

_____

2. What questions do you want your dream to answer? _____

_____

_____

_____

3. What method can you use to increase dream awareness or lucidity? _____

_____

_____

_____

4. How can your dreams guide your personal growth or transformation? _____

_____

_____

_____

5. How will you reflect on your dreams upon waking? _____

_____

_____

Dreaming Intentions

Date: _____ Dream Intention: _____

1. What is your intention for tonight's dream, what insights do you seek? _____

_____
_____
_____

2. What questions do you want your dream to answer? _____

_____
_____
_____

3. What method can you use to increase dream awareness or lucidity? _____

_____
_____
_____

4. How can your dreams guide your personal growth or transformation? _____

_____
_____
_____

5. How will you reflect on your dreams upon waking? _____

_____
_____

Dreaming Intentions

Date: _____ Dream Intention: _____

1. What is your intention for tonight's dream, what insights do you seek? _____

_____
_____
_____
_____

2. What questions do you want your dream to answer? _____

_____
_____
_____

3. What method can you use to increase dream awareness or lucidity? _____

_____
_____
_____

4. How can your dreams guide your personal growth or transformation? _____

_____
_____
_____

5. How will you reflect on your dreams upon waking? _____

_____
_____

witchcraftspellsmagick.com

Dream Journal

Dreaming Intentions

Date: _____ Dream Intention: _____

1. What is your intention for tonight's dream, what insights do you seek? _____

_____

_____

_____

2. What questions do you want your dream to answer? _____

_____

_____

_____

3. What method can you use to increase dream awareness or lucidity? _____

_____

_____

_____

4. How can your dreams guide your personal growth or transformation? _____

_____

_____

_____

5. How will you reflect on your dreams upon waking? _____

_____

_____

Dreaming Intentions

Date: _____ Dream Intention: _____

1. What is your intention for tonight's dream, what insights do you seek? _____

2. What questions do you want your dream to answer? _____

3. What method can you use to increase dream awareness or lucidity? _____

4. How can your dreams guide your personal growth or transformation? _____

5. How will you reflect on your dreams upon waking? _____

Dream Journal 191

Dreaming Intentions

Date: _____ Dream Intention: _____

1. What is your intention for tonight's dream, what insights do you seek? _____

2. What questions do you want your dream to answer? _____

3. What method can you use to increase dream awareness or lucidity? _____

4. How can your dreams guide your personal growth or transformation? _____

5. How will you reflect on your dreams upon waking? _____

Dreaming Intentions

Date: _____ Dream Intention: _____

1. What is your intention for tonight's dream, what insights do you seek? _____

_____

_____

_____

2. What questions do you want your dream to answer? _____

_____

_____

3. What method can you use to increase dream awareness or lucidity? _____

_____

_____

4. How can your dreams guide your personal growth or transformation? _____

_____

_____

5. How will you reflect on your dreams upon waking? _____

_____

_____

Dream Journal

Dreaming Intentions

Date: _____ Dream Intention: _____

1. What is your intention for tonight's dream, what insights do you seek? _____

_____
_____
_____

2. What questions do you want your dream to answer? _____

_____
_____
_____

3. What method can you use to increase dream awareness or lucidity? _____

_____
_____
_____

4. How can your dreams guide your personal growth or transformation? _____

_____
_____
_____

5. How will you reflect on your dreams upon waking? _____

_____
_____

Dreaming Intentions

Date: _____ Dream Intention: _____

1. What is your intention for tonight's dream, what insights do you seek? _____

_____
_____
_____
_____
_____

2. What questions do you want your dream to answer? _____

_____
_____
_____
_____

3. What method can you use to increase dream awareness or lucidity? _____

_____
_____
_____
_____

4. How can your dreams guide your personal growth or transformation? _____

_____
_____
_____
_____

5. How will you reflect on your dreams upon waking? _____

_____
_____
_____

witchcraftspellsmagick.com

Dream Journal

Dreaming Intentions

Date: _____ Dream Intention: _____

1. What is your intention for tonight's dream, what insights do you seek? _____

_____

_____

_____

2. What questions do you want your dream to answer? _____

_____

_____

_____

3. What method can you use to increase dream awareness or lucidity? _____

_____

_____

_____

4. How can your dreams guide your personal growth or transformation? _____

_____

_____

_____

5. How will you reflect on your dreams upon waking? _____

_____

_____

Dreaming Intentions

Date: _____ Dream Intention: _____

1. What is your intention for tonight's dream, what insights do you seek? _____

_____

_____

_____

_____

2. What questions do you want your dream to answer? _____

_____

_____

_____

3. What method can you use to increase dream awareness or lucidity? _____

_____

_____

_____

4. How can your dreams guide your personal growth or transformation? _____

_____

_____

_____

5. How will you reflect on your dreams upon waking? _____

_____

_____

Dream Journal   203

Dreaming Intentions

Date: _____ Dream Intention: _____

1. What is your intention for tonight's dream, what insights do you seek? _____

_____

_____

_____

2. What questions do you want your dream to answer? _____

_____

_____

_____

3. What method can you use to increase dream awareness or lucidity? _____

_____

_____

_____

4. How can your dreams guide your personal growth or transformation? _____

_____

_____

_____

5. How will you reflect on your dreams upon waking? _____

_____

_____

Dreaming Intentions

Date: _____ Dream Intention: _____

1. What is your intention for tonight's dream, what insights do you seek? _____

2. What questions do you want your dream to answer? _____

3. What method can you use to increase dream awareness or lucidity? _____

4. How can your dreams guide your personal growth or transformation? _____

5. How will you reflect on your dreams upon waking? _____

Dream Journal

Dreaming Intentions

Date: _____ Dream Intention: _____

1. What is your intention for tonight's dream, what insights do you seek? _____

_____
_____
_____

2. What questions do you want your dream to answer? _____

_____
_____
_____

3. What method can you use to increase dream awareness or lucidity? _____

_____
_____
_____

4. How can your dreams guide your personal growth or transformation? _____

_____
_____
_____

5. How will you reflect on your dreams upon waking? _____

_____
_____

Dreaming Intentions

Date: _____ Dream Intention: _____

1. What is your intention for tonight's dream, what insights do you seek? _____

_____
_____
_____
_____

2. What questions do you want your dream to answer? _____

_____
_____
_____
_____

3. What method can you use to increase dream awareness or lucidity? _____

_____
_____
_____
_____

4. How can your dreams guide your personal growth or transformation? _____

_____
_____
_____
_____

5. How will you reflect on your dreams upon waking? _____

_____
_____

Dream Journal

witchcraftspellsmagick.com

Dreaming Intentions

Date: _____ Dream Intention: _____

1. What is your intention for tonight's dream, what insights do you seek? _____

_____

_____

_____

2. What questions do you want your dream to answer? _____

_____

_____

_____

3. What method can you use to increase dream awareness or lucidity? _____

_____

_____

_____

4. How can your dreams guide your personal growth or transformation? _____

_____

_____

_____

5. How will you reflect on your dreams upon waking? _____

_____

_____

Dreaming Intentions

Date: _____ Dream Intention: _____

1. What is your intention for tonight's dream, what insights do you seek? _____

_____

_____

_____

_____

2. What questions do you want your dream to answer? _____

_____

_____

_____

3. What method can you use to increase dream awareness or lucidity? _____

_____

_____

_____

4. How can your dreams guide your personal growth or transformation? _____

_____

_____

_____

5. How will you reflect on your dreams upon waking? _____

_____

_____

Dream Journal

witchcraftspellsmagick.com

Dreaming Intentions

Date: _____ Dream Intention: _____

1. What is your intention for tonight's dream, what insights do you seek? _____

_____

_____

_____

_____

2. What questions do you want your dream to answer? _____

_____

_____

_____

3. What method can you use to increase dream awareness or lucidity? _____

_____

_____

_____

4. How can your dreams guide your personal growth or transformation? _____

_____

_____

_____

5. How will you reflect on your dreams upon waking? _____

_____

_____

PART 5 | EVENING

Lucid Dreaming Log
Heightened Dreaming Awareness

Lucid dreaming occurs when you are aware of your thoughts, actions, and surroundings in an alternate state of consciousness, often during sleep.

Your heightened awareness allows you to consciously engage with the dream world, guiding your experiences and exploring your subconscious mind. Lucid dreaming techniques enhance your ability to recognize and control your state of consciousness, whether you're dreaming, meditating, or in any other altered mental state.

Lucid Dreaming Techniques:
Dreaming, Meditation, Scrying, Breath Work, Trance States, Ritual, Chanting or Mantras, Spinning, Dancing or Movement, Drumming, Hypnosis, Visualization

How to use your Lucid Dreaming Tracker
Date: Record the date the dream occurred.
Dream Name: A brief name to trigger your memory.
Description/Summary: Use this space to capture the narrative of your dream.
Lucid Techniques Used: Note the methods used to achieve lucidity.
Outcome/Insights: Reflect on your experiences, and on any lessons you learned.

Recommended Reading:
'The Art of Dreaming' by Carlos Castaneda
'Lucid Dreaming: A Concise Guide to Awakening in Your Dreams and in Your Life' by Stephen LaBerge
'The Tibetan Yogas of Dream and Sleep' by Tenzin Wangyal Rinpoche

Lucid Dreaming
Techniques & Methods...

Lucid dreaming offers the ability to become aware of and control your dreams. To help you reach this state, here are several techniques that will guide you.

Breath Work: Deep, rhythmic breathing such as belly breathing or alternate nostril breathing calms the mind and body, making it easier to enter a lucid state.

Chanting or Mantras: Repeating mantras or affirmations, such as *"I will know when I am dreaming,"* helps imprint the intention to achieve lucidity into your subconscious mind.

Dancing or Movement: Engaging in rhythmic movement, like dancing, raises your energy levels and heightens awareness, increasing the likelihood of lucidity.

Drumming: The repetitive beats of drumming can alter brainwave frequencies, shifting your consciousness to a more aware state during sleep.

Dream Journaling: Writing down your dreams daily enhances recall, helping you recognize patterns and triggers for lucidity, when you are dreaming.

Energy Flow and Balance: Before sleep, focus on balancing your energy through visualization or light breath work. Imagine your energy flowing freely, clearing blockages. This enhances your awareness, potentially increasing lucidity.

Hypnosis: Self-hypnosis or guided hypnosis can be a powerful way to induce lucidity. These techniques train your mind to recognize when you're dreaming and empower you to take control.

Meditation: Meditation clears the mind and enhances awareness, helping maintain lucidity while you sleep. Practicing mindfulness increases your chances of becoming aware in your dreams.

witchcraftspellsmagick.com

Mnemonic Induction of Lucid Dreams (MILD): MILD involves setting the intention to recognize when you're dreaming. Try brain training by repeating a mantra as you fall asleep: *"Consciously dream, knowing I am dreaming."*

Reality Checks: Frequently checking your surroundings during the day—looking at your hands, reading text, or pushing a finger through your palm—trains your brain to recognize when you're dreaming.

Ritual: A pre-sleep ritual, such as lighting candles or casting a circle, signals your subconscious that you're entering a lucid dream practice and helps create mental space for lucidity.

Scrying: Using tools like a scrying mirror or crystal ball before sleep can help focus your intention for lucid dreaming, serving as visual anchors for your subconscious.

Heightened Sensory Awareness
By becoming more aware of subtle physical sensations in your body as you fall asleep, you can enhance your ability to enter a lucid state. Pay attention to the feeling of your body becoming heavy or light, or the sensations of relaxation in your muscles. These physical cues can act as signals that you are transitioning into sleep, helping you recognize when you are about to enter a dream.

Spinning: Spinning in place during a dream is a common technique for triggering lucidity. The sensation of spinning helps you recognize that you are dreaming.

Trance States: Inducing light trance states using self-hypnosis, relaxation, or guided visualization can prime your mind for lucidity and help it stay aware while you dream.

Visualization: Imagine yourself lucid, hold the feeling as you enter the dream state. Mentally rehearsing lucidity strengthens the connection between your conscious and subconscious, enhancing your ability to achieve it while dreaming.

Lucid Dreaming Log *Example*

Date: 11th February   Dream Name: The Veil of Stars

Lucid Techniques Used: Dream Journaling (Morning reflection)
Chanting Mantras (Divine illumination)

Experiences: Before sleep, I spent time reflecting on my dreams from the previous night, which set the intention for tonight's journey. As I lay down, I repeated a mantra: "I am the keeper of the veil, and the stars are my guide." In the dream, I was walking through a vast, celestial plane, where constellations shifted and formed symbols of power. I became lucid when the stars aligned into a sigil, and I knew I could shape the dream's outcome.

Outcome/Insights: The sigil formed in the stars revealed an ancient connection to wisdom and power. The chant deepened my connection to the astral realm, and the dream illuminated the path I must take in waking life. It reminded me that the divine is always present, guiding me through the veil of illusion into the truth beyond.

Lucid Dreaming Log *Example*

Date: 13th February   Dream Name: The Altar of Shadows

Lucid Techniques Used: Breath Work (Alternate nostril breathing) (Visualization (Third eye focus)

Experiences: I began the night with deep, rhythmic breath work, channeling energy through my body. As I fell asleep, I visualized a glowing third eye. In the dream, I found myself in a dimly lit temple surrounded by shadowy figures. I realized I was dreaming when I touched the altar and felt a surge of energy. I focused on grounding myself, invoking clarity through the breath, and was able to control my movements within the dream.

Outcome/Insights: This dream felt like a spiritual initiation. The shadowy figures represented hidden aspects of my psyche, and the altar symbolized my ability to manifest my will. The breath work and visualization helped me stay present and aware, reminding me that clarity and control come from within, even in the face of the unknown.

Lucid Dreaming Log

Date: _____ Dream Name: _____

Lucid Techniques Used: _____

_____

Experiences: _____

_____

_____

_____

_____

_____

Outcome/Insights: _____

_____

_____

_____

_____

Lucid Dreaming Log

Date: _____ Dream Name: _____

Lucid Techniques Used: _____

Experiences: _____

Outcome/Insights: _____

Lucid Dreaming Log

Date: _____ Dream Name: _____

Lucid Techniques Used: _____

_____

Experiences: _____

_____

_____

_____

_____

Outcome/Insights: _____

_____

_____

_____

Lucid Dreaming Log

Date: _____ Dream Name: _____

Lucid Techniques Used: _____

Experiences: _____

Outcome/Insights: _____

"Four days will quickly
steep themselves in nights;
Four nights will quickly
dream away the time."
– William Shakespeare *author A Midsummer Night's Dream*

witchcraftspellsmagick.com

Lucid Dreaming Log

Date: _____ Dream Name: _____

Lucid Techniques Used: _____

_____

Experiences: _____

_____

_____

_____

_____

_____

Outcome/Insights: _____

_____

_____

_____

Lucid Dreaming Log

Date: _____ Dream Name: _____

Lucid Techniques Used: _____

_____

Experiences: _____

_____

_____

_____

_____

_____

Outcome/Insights: _____

_____

_____

_____

_____

Lucid Dreaming Log

Date: _____ Dream Name: _____

Lucid Techniques Used: _____

Experiences: _____

Outcome/Insights: _____

Lucid Dreaming Log

Date: _____ Dream Name: _____

Lucid Techniques Used: _____

_____

Experiences: _____

_____

_____

_____

_____

Outcome/Insights: _____

_____

_____

_____

Lucid Dreaming Log

Date: _____ Dream Name: _____

Lucid Techniques Used: _____

Experiences: _____

Outcome/Insights: _____

Lucid Dreaming Log

Date: _____ Dream Name: _____

Lucid Techniques Used: _____

_____

Experiences: _____

_____

_____

_____

_____

Outcome/Insights: _____

_____

_____

_____

Lucid Dreaming Log

Date: _____ Dream Name: _____

Lucid Techniques Used: _____

Experiences: _____

Outcome/Insights: _____

"Say," said a small and hairy voice in his ear, "but would you mind dreamin' a bit quieter?"
– Neil Gaiman *author Stardust*

witchcraftspellsmagick.com

Lucid Dreaming Log

Date: _____ Dream Name: _____

Lucid Techniques Used: _____

_____

Experiences: _____

_____

_____

_____

_____

Outcome/Insights: _____

_____

_____

_____

Lucid Dreaming Log

Date: _____ Dream Name: _____

Lucid Techniques Used: _____

_____

Experiences: _____

_____

_____

_____

_____

Outcome/Insights: _____

_____

_____

_____

Lucid Dreaming Log

Date: _____ Dream Name: _____

Lucid Techniques Used: _____

_____

Experiences: _____

_____

_____

_____

_____

_____

Outcome/Insights: _____

_____

_____

_____

Lucid Dreaming Log

Date: _____ Dream Name: _____

Lucid Techniques Used: _____

_____

Experiences: _____

_____

_____

_____

_____

_____

Outcome/Insights: _____

_____

_____

_____

_____

Lucid Dreaming Log

Date: _____ Dream Name: _____

Lucid Techniques Used: _____

_____

Experiences: _____

_____

_____

_____

_____

_____

Outcome/Insights: _____

_____

_____

_____

_____

Lucid Dreaming Log

Date: _____ Dream Name: _____

Lucid Techniques Used: _____

_____

Experiences: _____

_____

_____

_____

_____

_____

Outcome/Insights: _____

_____

_____

_____

_____

witchcraftspellsmagick.com

Lucid Dreaming Log

Date: _____ Dream Name: _____

Lucid Techniques Used: _____

_____

Experiences: _____

_____

_____

_____

_____

Outcome/Insights: _____

_____

_____

_____

> "Life,
> what is it
> but a dream?"
> – Lewis Carroll *author Through the Looking Glass*

witchcraftspellsmagick.com

Lucid Dreaming Log

Date: _____ Dream Name: _____

Lucid Techniques Used: _____

Experiences: _____

Outcome/Insights: _____

Lucid Dreaming Log

Date: _____ Dream Name: _____

Lucid Techniques Used: _____

Experiences: _____

_____

_____

_____

_____

Outcome/Insights: _____

_____

_____

_____

Lucid Dreaming Log

Date: _____ Dream Name: _____

Lucid Techniques Used: _____

_____

Experiences: _____

_____

_____

_____

_____

_____

Outcome/Insights: _____

_____

_____

_____

Lucid Dreaming Log

Date: _____ Dream Name: _____

Lucid Techniques Used: _____

_____

Experiences: _____

_____

_____

_____

_____

_____

Outcome/Insights: _____

_____

_____

_____

_____

Lucid Dreaming Log

Date: _____ Dream Name: _____

Lucid Techniques Used: _____

Experiences: _____

_____

_____

_____

_____

Outcome/Insights: _____

_____

_____

_____

Lucid Dreaming Log

Date: _____ Dream Name: _____

Lucid Techniques Used: _____

_____

Experiences: _____

_____

_____

_____

_____

_____

Outcome/Insights: _____

_____

_____

_____

_____

Lucid Dreaming Log

Date: _____ Dream Name: _____

Lucid Techniques Used: _____

Experiences: _____

Outcome/Insights: _____

PART 6 | EVENING

Dream Flow
Creative Dream Flow Journaling

By journaling, doodling, writing, listing, or visualizing through your conscious mind, you invite specific themes, emotions, and symbols into your subconscious ultimately guiding your dreams.

The practice of 'Dream Flow Journaling' should be led by your subconscious while awake, allowing free expression through intuitive lines, words, or shapes. This process deepens your connection to the dream world, nurturing the flow of insights and personal growth that naturally align with your journey.

Drawing inspiration from the Dreaming Intentions section, journaling at this stage expands upon the focused intentions set before sleep, allowing the subconscious to continue the dialogue with your conscious mind. By integrating free space journaling, you invite a deeper exploration of the dream world, uncovering meaningful experiences and insights.

This section provides prompts to help you set purposeful, focused intentions for your dreams, enhancing the exploration and reflection process.

Set Intentions for Your Dreams
Journal your primary intention for tonight's dream.
Use the following pages to explore areas for growth, change, awakening, or any themes or questions you'd like to address in your dreams.

Dream Flow Journaling

Journal your primary intention for tonight's dream

Use the following pages to explore areas for growth, change, awakening, or any themes or questions you'd like to address in your dreams.

Dream Flow Journaling

Journal your primary intention for tonight's dream
Use the following pages to explore areas for growth, change, awakening, or any themes or questions you'd like to address in your dreams.

Dream Flow Journaling

Journal your primary intention for tonight's dream

Use the following pages to explore areas for growth, change, awakening, or any themes or questions you'd like to address in your dreams.

witchcraftspellsmagick.com

Dream Flow Journaling

Journal your primary intention for tonight's dream
Use the following pages to explore areas for growth, change, awakening, or any themes or questions you'd like to address in your dreams.

Dream Flow Journaling

Journal your primary intention for tonight's dream

Use the following pages to explore areas for growth, change, awakening, or any themes or questions you'd like to address in your dreams.

Dream Flow Journaling

Journal your primary intention for tonight's dream

Use the following pages to explore areas for growth, change, awakening, or any themes or questions you'd like to address in your dreams.

Dream Flow Journaling

Journal your primary intention for tonight's dream

Use the following pages to explore areas for growth, change, awakening, or any themes or questions you'd like to address in your dreams.

Dream Flow Journaling

Journal your primary intention for tonight's dream

Use the following pages to explore areas for growth, change, awakening, or any themes or questions you'd like to address in your dreams.

Dream Flow Journaling

Journal your primary intention for tonight's dream

Use the following pages to explore areas for growth, change, awakening, or any themes or questions you'd like to address in your dreams.

Dream Flow Journaling

Journal your primary intention for tonight's dream
Use the following pages to explore areas for growth, change, awakening, or any themes or questions you'd like to address in your dreams.

Dream Flow Journaling

Journal your primary intention for tonight's dream

Use the following pages to explore areas for growth, change, awakening, or any themes or questions you'd like to address in your dreams.

Dream Flow Journaling

Journal your primary intention for tonight's dream

Use the following pages to explore areas for growth, change, awakening, or any themes or questions you'd like to address in your dreams.

Dream Flow Journaling

Journal your primary intention for tonight's dream

Use the following pages to explore areas for growth, change, awakening, or any themes or questions you'd like to address in your dreams.

Dream Flow Journaling

Journal your primary intention for tonight's dream

Use the following pages to explore areas for growth, change, awakening, or any themes or questions you'd like to address in your dreams.

"Never go to sleep without
a request to your subconscious."
– Thomas Edison *inventor and businessman*

witchcraftspellsmagick.com

Dream Flow Journaling

Journal your primary intention for tonight's dream

Use the following pages to explore areas for growth, change, awakening, or any themes or questions you'd like to address in your dreams.

Dream Flow Journaling

Journal your primary intention for tonight's dream

Use the following pages to explore areas for growth, change, awakening, or any themes or questions you'd like to address in your dreams.

Dream Flow Journaling

Journal your primary intention for tonight's dream

Use the following pages to explore areas for growth, change, awakening, or any themes or questions you'd like to address in your dreams.

Dream Flow Journaling

Journal your primary intention for tonight's dream

Use the following pages to explore areas for growth, change, awakening, or any themes or questions you'd like to address in your dreams.

Dream Flow Journaling

Journal your primary intention for tonight's dream
Use the following pages to explore areas for growth, change, awakening, or any themes or questions you'd like to address in your dreams.

Dream Flow Journaling

Journal your primary intention for tonight's dream

Use the following pages to explore areas for growth, change, awakening, or any themes or questions you'd like to address in your dreams.

Dream Flow Journaling

Journal your primary intention for tonight's dream

Use the following pages to explore areas for growth, change, awakening, or any themes or questions you'd like to address in your dreams.

Dream Flow Journaling

Journal your primary intention for tonight's dream

Use the following pages to explore areas for growth, change, awakening, or any themes or questions you'd like to address in your dreams.

Dream Flow Journaling

Journal your primary intention for tonight's dream

Use the following pages to explore areas for growth, change, awakening, or any themes or questions you'd like to address in your dreams.

Dream Flow Journaling

Journal your primary intention for tonight's dream

Use the following pages to explore areas for growth, change, awakening, or any themes or questions you'd like to address in your dreams.

Dream Flow Journaling

Journal your primary intention for tonight's dream
Use the following pages to explore areas for growth, change, awakening, or any themes or questions you'd like to address in your dreams.

Dream Flow Journaling

Journal your primary intention for tonight's dream

Use the following pages to explore areas for growth, change, awakening, or any themes or questions you'd like to address in your dreams.

Dream Flow Journaling

Journal your primary intention for tonight's dream
Use the following pages to explore areas for growth, change, awakening, or any themes or questions you'd like to address in your dreams.

Dream Flow Journaling

Journal your primary intention for tonight's dream

Use the following pages to explore areas for growth, change, awakening, or any themes or questions you'd like to address in your dreams.

Dream Flow Journaling

Journal your primary intention for tonight's dream

Use the following pages to explore areas for growth, change, awakening, or any themes or questions you'd like to address in your dreams.

"If you live in a past dream,
you don't enjoy what is happening
right now because you will always
wish it to be different than it is."
– Don Miguel Ruiz *author Four Agreements:*
A Practical Guide to Personal Freedom

witchcraftspellsmagick.com

Dream Flow Journaling

Journal your primary intention for tonight's dream
Use the following pages to explore areas for growth, change, awakening, or any themes or questions you'd like to address in your dreams.

Dream Flow Journaling

Journal your primary intention for tonight's dream

Use the following pages to explore areas for growth, change, awakening, or any themes or questions you'd like to address in your dreams.

Dream Flow Journaling

Journal your primary intention for tonight's dream
Use the following pages to explore areas for growth, change, awakening, or any themes or questions you'd like to address in your dreams.

Dream Flow Journaling

Journal your primary intention for tonight's dream

Use the following pages to explore areas for growth, change, awakening, or any themes or questions you'd like to address in your dreams.

Dream Flow Journaling

Journal your primary intention for tonight's dream

Use the following pages to explore areas for growth, change, awakening, or any themes or questions you'd like to address in your dreams.

Dream Flow Journaling

Journal your primary intention for tonight's dream

Use the following pages to explore areas for growth, change, awakening, or any themes or questions you'd like to address in your dreams.

Dream Flow Journaling

Journal your primary intention for tonight's dream

Use the following pages to explore areas for growth, change, awakening, or any themes or questions you'd like to address in your dreams.

Dream Flow Journaling

Journal your primary intention for tonight's dream

Use the following pages to explore areas for growth, change, awakening, or any themes or questions you'd like to address in your dreams.

Dream Flow Journaling

Journal your primary intention for tonight's dream
Use the following pages to explore areas for growth, change, awakening, or any themes or questions you'd like to address in your dreams.

Dream Flow Journaling

Journal your primary intention for tonight's dream

Use the following pages to explore areas for growth, change, awakening, or any themes or questions you'd like to address in your dreams.

Dream Flow Journaling

Journal your primary intention for tonight's dream
Use the following pages to explore areas for growth, change, awakening, or any themes or questions you'd like to address in your dreams.

Dream Flow Journaling

Journal your primary intention for tonight's dream

Use the following pages to explore areas for growth, change, awakening, or any themes or questions you'd like to address in your dreams.

witchcraftspellsmagick.com

Dream Flow Journaling

Journal your primary intention for tonight's dream
Use the following pages to explore areas for growth, change, awakening, or any themes or questions you'd like to address in your dreams.

Dream Flow Journaling

Journal your primary intention for tonight's dream

Use the following pages to explore areas for growth, change, awakening, or any themes or questions you'd like to address in your dreams.

Dream Flow Journaling

Journal your primary intention for tonight's dream
Use the following pages to explore areas for growth, change, awakening, or any themes or questions you'd like to address in your dreams.

Bibliography
Recommended Reads

This bibliography is a curated list of essential recommended books that will deepen your understanding of dream symbolism, their interpretation, and their spiritual and psychological significance.

These works bridge the gap between ancient wisdom and modern insights, offering valuable perspectives for personal and spiritual growth.

"The Art of Dreaming" by Carlos Castaneda
Explores the spiritual and practical aspects of dreaming, particularly in the context of shamanic practices, offering a unique perspective on how to consciously interact with dream states for personal growth and spiritual insight.

"The Interpretation of Dreams" by Sigmund Freud
The seminal work by Freud that introduces his theory of dreams as reflections of unconscious desires and conflicts.

"The Language of Dreams" by Patricia Garfield
Focuses on the universal language of dreams, offering insights into dream analysis from a psychologist's perspective. Garfield's work is renowned for blending clinical psychology with dream research, providing a rich understanding of how dreams convey hidden truths and emotional healing.

"Man and His Symbols" by Carl G. Jung
Suggested for deeper insights into the symbolism found in your dreams.

"The Psychology of the Transference" by Carl G. Jung
Explores the relationship dynamics within the psychoanalytical process, which can also apply to understanding the symbolic exchanges in dreams.

witchcraftspellsmagick.com

"The Complete Dictionary of Dreams" by Dr. Michael Lennox
Provides comprehensive interpretations of dream symbols.
Also recommended for comprehensive interpretations of dream symbols.

"The Dreamer's Dictionary" by Stearn Robinson & Tom Corbett
A guide for interpreting the various symbols that appear in dreams.
Also mentioned as a reference for understanding dream symbols
and their meanings.

"Dreams and Spirituality: A Guide to the Soul's Journey" by John A. Sanford
Explores the connection between dreams and spiritual growth.
Also suggested for integrating dream insights with spiritual practice.

"The Witch's Book of Dreams" by Rose Vanden Eynden
Focuses on how witches can interpret and utilize dreams in their practices.
Recommended for those specifically interested in the intersection
of witchcraft and dream interpretation.

"Women's Symbols" by Barbara Walker
A comprehensive exploration of symbols associated with aspects and energies
in your dreams. This book provides insights into how these symbols manifest
in your subconscious and their significancein dream interpretation, particularly
in the context of exploring personal identity and spiritual growth.

"Dreams: A Portal to the Source" by Edward C. Whitmont
Recommended for exploring the connection between your dreams
and your unconscious.

"The Symbolic Quest" by Edward C. Whitmont
Provides insights into the symbolic expressions found in personal
and collective unconscious material, including dreams.

Witchcraft Spells Magick
witchcraftspellsmagick.com

WITCHCRAFT ACADEMY
Teaching Witches their Craft

Private Coven Group

Your invitation to Join!

witchcraftspellsmagick.com/pages/coven

www.ingramcontent.com/pod-product-compliance
Lightning Source LLC
Chambersburg PA
CBHW061733070526
44585CB00024B/2651